THE ONENESS CIRCLE HANDBOOK

*A Guide for Evolving Spiritual Growth in a
Supportive and Structured Group Environment*

Carol B. Stanley

Masters of Education
Licensed Professional Clinical Counselor Supervisor

Stacie Will

Masters of Education

BALBOA.
PRESS

A DIVISION OF HAY HOUSE

Cover art and design by Gail Wetherell-Sack.

Carol and Stacie may be available to assist you in launching your Oneness Circle.
Different tiers of support are available.
For further information contact:
Carol B. Stanley
CarolStanley330@gmail.com

Stacie Will
stacie@mindfullyaligned.com

Balboa Press books may be ordered through booksellers or by contacting:

Balboa Press
A Division of Hay House
1663 Liberty Drive
Bloomington, IN 47403
www.balboapress.com
1 (877) 407-4847

ISBN: 978-1-5043-4541-5 (sc)
ISBN: 978-1-5043-4542-2 (e)

Library of Congress Control Number: 2015920221

Print information available on the last page.

Balboa Press rev. date: 1/13/2016

to
Melinda
a light in our lives

TABLE OF CONTENTS

ACKNOWLEDGEMENTS

We wish to express our deep affection and appreciation to each Oneness Circle member for accepting that first invitation and for being an enthusiastic, compassionate, and inspiring participant. Thank you Terri Hooper, Connie Isle, Loren Keith, Melinda Keith, JoAnne Pinkerton, and Heather Popio; it has been a life-transforming journey filled with heart-felt connections. You are very much present in this handbook.

Special recognition goes out to our three literary angels with insightful, skillful editing gifts. We extend our profound gratitude to Jane Eckert, Ph.D., Melinda Keith, and Vince Lisi for your clarity of language and spiritual vision.

To artist friend, Gail Wetherell-Sack, we thank you for the illuminating cover that captures the essence of the pages within. We recognize that art is your sanctuary, your place of peace, healing and joy.

We express our love and gratitude to our spouses, James Stanley and John Bullock, for lovingly nurturing us as we guided this handbook from conception to completion.

We gratefully acknowledge the writers and speakers we have quoted for their wisdom and inspiration.

And, above all, we are grateful for the inspiration and influence of <u>A Course In Miracles</u> on this handbook, and for our weekly teacher, Vince Lisi, for being a light on our path.

INTRODUCTION

"We share a common purpose…
to be aligned and share a single vision of Oneness,
co-creating wherever we are.
The Oneness is guiding each one of us.
We do this diversely and uniquely."
Vince Lisi

"You see, Pluto, the atoms that make up all life on Earth came
from the same stars that make up everything
in our solar system - moons, planets, and even you.
We all share the same origins and we are all connected,
because the entire universe lives within us all."
Neil deGrasse Tyson

Welcome to The Oneness Circle Handbook. We have come together to share a process with you that we call The Oneness Circle. The Oneness Circle is a structured meeting of people who want to evolve their spiritual growth in a supportive environment of shared information and inspiration.

We believe there is great wisdom within all of us. This wisdom expresses itself in the form of Prompts, those individual expressions that come from our inner being. As we go within aligning our mind, body, and heart with the present moment, we allow the flow of this guidance and direction.

It is through this practice of listening to our inner voice and allowing it to blossom into expression that our inner guidance flows creatively, lovingly, and powerfully. As we join with other like-minded individuals, we gain confidence in our ability to hear the wisdom within and follow its direction.

The Oneness Circle process assists us to embrace the universal truth that there is no separation between us, and that we are all part of the same energy called Oneness. Together, we support each other in living our highest and best selves.

Our inspiration has come from the visions of Barbara Marx Hubbard, author of Emergence; Rasha, author of Oneness; the affirmation principles of Louise Hay; and the Mastermind process of Jack Boland.

Further inspiration has come from Vince Lisi whose empowering enlightenment teachings and practices combined with his commitment to our personal evolution have nurtured our connection to the Oneness energy.

We invite you to create your own Oneness Circle. We offer this process with love, knowing you are one with the power that created you.

Namasté.

"A new species is arising on the planet.
It is arising now, and you are it."
Eckhart Tolle

May the reading of what our founding Oneness Circle members have expressed about their participation in the group offer further inspiration and encouragement to form a Oneness Circle of your own.

"The group guides me to positive manifestations through writing and discussing whatever is prompting me to move forward on my path. Each month as I listen to others and see their lives unfold, I am encouraged to do the same. We are filled with joy as we hear others sharing the miracles in their lives. It gives us all courage. Each of us has grown spiritually by being a part of the group." – **Connie**

"Being a part of a Oneness Circle has been a blessing in my life. I have participated in the Oneness Circle for over three years and am reminded constantly of the importance of coming together with caring and like-minded individuals to share miracles as well as prompts. Carol and Stacie have developed this structured, consistent Oneness Circle handbook to help guide this process. It gives the agenda, timeline for the meeting, 10 steps, as well as procedure for participants to feel free and comfortable sharing.

"Participants share their miracles that have happened since the last meeting. This encourages participants to focus, notice, and remember all of the miracles and manifestations throughout the month. Just as important is the sharing of prompts and framing them in affirmations as a way to focus on what we want to attract. During this time of sharing, the participants are both giving and receiving from the heart, as others hold that sacred space for what is difficult to believe alone. With our spiritual partners there is a strength that opens the doorway for growth, beliefs, and affirmations to be expanded, visualized, and actualized. The clear and concise 10 steps celebrate the positive direction of the affirmations.

"This union of spiritual friends continues to help me remember what Jesus said: 'Where two or three are gathered in my name, there am I in the midst of them.' By coming together for this spiritual journey, each individual realizes the gift of two or more and the blessing to all." – **JoAnne**

"I learned to reveal my heartfelt feelings with this group. As I focus on sharing my blessings and affirmations, I feel a family-like sense of support from each of the members. I feel grateful and blessed to be part of the Oneness Circle." – **Loren**

"My participation in our Oneness Circle has changed me. I have learned to listen ever more carefully to my heart/internal center. The format encourages sharing heart prompts with the group and then affirming that they are happening. We encourage and celebrate each member's path and growth. Through this process we each are manifesting our inner wisdom. I have come to know that my evolution involves living in my Higher Self and experiencing the Oneness we all share. This group experience feeds and nourishes that evolution.

"Learn to listen to your heart's wisdom and desire
Walk with me in Oneness
Find your path
Saunter with like-minded souls
Skip with joy" – **Melinda**

"This group made all the difference in nurturing my understanding of positive affirmations and the ability to raise the energy level of my intentions and desires of my heart. When an affirmation is shared then reaffirmed back to me by each loving member of the group, the energy of the affirmation increases exponentially. Until joining this group I had not really thought of prompts as more than simply ideas flitting through a very active brain. I had not really appreciated what can be manifested on a daily basis by tapping into the power of Oneness energy. I continue to marvel at this process!" – **Terri**

CHAPTER 1

THE ONENESS CIRCLE

"We are Oneness…
We are as a drop of water is to the ocean –
bonded in Oneness to it,
being of it, and unto it,
yet having identity and self-perception."
Rasha

"The energetic exchange that occurs
when two or more align at the essential level
illuminates and activates human intelligence."
Barbara Marx Hubbard

VISION OF THE ONENESS CIRCLE

Oneness: An awareness and knowing that we have the energy of the Source within us. This energy is our connection to each other, to all that is, and to the Source.

According to the teachings of enlightenment principles, there are two parts of me:

> The part of me that is the Divine within, my true nature, we call my Higher Self or Big Me. It is the eternal, changeless, perfect part of myself connected to all that is and to the human part of me.

> The part of me that includes my body as well as my mind, emotions, and life circumstances such as possessions, social status, and occupation, we call the human part of me or my little me.

As we align the human qualities of our little me with the power and direction of our Big Me/Higher Self, we can experience living life as an integrated being, co-creating with the guidance of Oneness energy within.

Higher Self communicates through Prompts and uses dynamic energy through the physical body, mind, and emotions to interact with the physical world.

Through the experience of the Oneness Circle, we make the commitment to our personal evolution and join with others who are dedicated to this process. Our experience of our connection to the Oneness energy expands and grows within each of us.

The Oneness Circle creates an environment of sharing and inspiration as we open to one another, listen with our whole being, and echo back from our hearts. It nurtures a community of support and encouragement to one another in listening to our Prompts and following their guidance.

The inspiration and power that come with meeting and co-creating as a group are very meaningful. As Thich Nhat Hanh said, "Without community we cannot go very far." And as Jesus said, "Where two or three are gathered in my name, there am I in the midst of them."

"To reinforce the inner experience, it is highly desirable to
seek out communion with two or more others -
to expand the Inner Sanctuary to include others."
Barbara Marx Hubbard

PURPOSE OF THE ONENESS CIRCLE

The Oneness Circle encourages evolving spiritual growth in a supportive and structured group environment.

Creating a Oneness Circle offers the opportunities to:

- Connect with like-minded individuals though creating and nurturing a community of support and sharing.
- Recognize Miracles and Manifestations that flow from inner guidance.
- Acknowledge inner guidance and wisdom as Prompts from Higher Self.
- Practice listening and responding to Prompts.
- Create Affirmations based on Prompts which energize co-creations.
- Express by sharing experiences of Miracles, Manifestations, Prompts, and Affirmations.
- Support and encourage members by listening and responding heartfully.
- Participate in and celebrate the Ten Steps of Expressing Affirmations.
- Experience spiritual intimacy in an environment of compassion and non-judgment.
- Develop confidence of the connection and expression of the Oneness energy within.

"We echo back to each other our essential selves.
We fall in love with one another at the essence level.
This experience vastly accelerates our own integration and emergence."
Barbara Marx Hubbard

"Do not hesitate to put out the call to others.
Share your experience. See whose heart it touches.
Others are waiting for you as you are waiting for them."
Barbara Marx Hubbard

COMMUNITY OF THE ONENESS CIRCLE

The Oneness Circle is a group of 3 to 6 people on a spiritual journey who make a commitment to meet regularly to support one another. The creation of a Oneness Circle is for members who are dedicated to the continued evolving spiritual growth of themselves, while supporting others doing the same. The Oneness Circle provides the opportunity to create a supportive and structured group environment to encourage and facilitate this process of connection and growth.

Oneness Circle members **ASPIRE** to:

- A path of evolving spiritual growth.
- A daily spiritual practice that may include meditation, prayer, focused breathing, yoga, qigong, tai chi, service to others, being in nature, music, dance, chanting, etc.
- Guidance, direction, and power from the Higher Self.
- Frequent expressions of gratitude.
- Recognition of the flow and synchronicity of life.
- An openness to understanding that there is meaning behind every event.
- A trust that everything is unfolding according to Divine order and timing for the highest and best good.
- A knowing that the benevolent universe is supportive as we unfold and manifest/co-create our heart's desires.
- Deep down happiness, joy, peace, bliss, internal contentment.
- A felt knowingness that we are loving and magnificent, and so is everyone else.

"I know who I am. I know who you are. I know why we are here on earth."
Vince Lisi

CHAPTER 2

CREATION OF THE ONENESS CIRCLE

"When the energy of the soul is
recognized, acknowledged, and valued,
it begins to infuse the life of the personality."
Gary Zukav

"Share with one another exactly
where you are in your own emergence,
offering gentle encouragement to one another."
Barbara Marx Hubbard

USING THE ONENESS CIRCLE HANDBOOK

This handbook has been created to provide a framework and structure of how to build and facilitate a Oneness Circle. Step by step guidance is given for each meeting. Suggestions of how to facilitate Oneness Circle sessions are included.

Typically, the Oneness Circle members meet monthly. Each meeting is based on a two-hour timeframe.

To get started, a minimum of three meetings is needed to learn the structure, develop core ideas, and implement the process. This handbook includes a combination of individual and group practices that develop the Oneness Circle process. Once established, the Oneness Circle is a reoccurring meeting.

There is no limit as to the number of meetings a group may have. At the time of publication, our Oneness Circle is in its fourth year together.

Each of the first three meetings is outlined in sequential order along with an estimated timeline. Suggestions for opening and closing the Oneness Circle meeting and detailed steps of how to prepare for the each session are included. Chapters 3, 4, and 5 contain this information on pages 15 to 52.

The appendix provides support in creating and participating in a Oneness Circle. It includes a letter of invitation, contact list, Oneness Circle Notes, sample Affirmations, examples of compiling Affirmations, glossary, resources, and wisdom and inspiration. The appendix can be found on pages 53 to 67.

Following the appendix is the section providing multiple copies of the Oneness Circle Notes form for use in future Oneness Circle meetings. These forms are located on pages 69 to 79.

For an overview of the first three Oneness Circle meetings and the appendix, please review the following pages 7 to 12.

To start preparing for the first Oneness Circle, please go to page 13.

"As you come to seek and see the virtues and strengths and nobilities of others,
you begin to seek and see them in yourself also."
Gary Zukav

The First Oneness Circle Meeting

The first meeting, as outlined in Chapter 3, serves as the orientation and introduction to the process of The Oneness Circle. It is a time for the group to connect with one another, build a foundation of community, and become familiar with the Oneness Circle philosophy.

Together the group will:

Pause to Meditate Using a Centering Technique.

The practice of quieting the mind and relaxing the body assists us with connecting to the present moment which in turn supports listening and responding heartfully and communicating through our Higher Self.

Establish Individual and Group Guidelines.

A community of trust and sharing is essential in facilitating meaningful Oneness Circle meetings. By establishing guidelines that are important to the group, sharing and growth are encouraged.

Discuss Responding to Life Circumstances.

As members engage in the Oneness Circle process, various situations of life may occur. A member may find his or her emotions to be reactive rather than responsive. Or someone may receive news that may make them question his or her connection with the Source. While the Oneness Circle is not a therapy session, members can support one another.

Introduce the Oneness Circle Process and Oneness Circle Notes.

A specific format for meeting is introduced that includes using and sharing the Oneness Circle Notes – a form for recording Miracles, Manifestations, Prompts, and Affirmations used throughout each session.

Discuss Miracles and Manifestations.

Miracles and Manifestations are defined, and examples of each are given. Group members are encouraged to reflect upon a personal experience.

Prepare for the Second Oneness Circle Meeting.

Date, time, host, and location of the next Oneness Circle meeting are discussed. Home practice and preparation as well as readings from <u>The Oneness Circle Handbook</u> are reviewed.

Close the Oneness Circle Session.

The meeting concludes with a closing ritual.

"…wise and compassionate guidance is always available to you."
Gary Zukav

The Second Oneness Circle Meeting

The second meeting, as outlined in Chapter 4, will continue the process of guiding the members in defining key concepts and terminology of the Oneness Circle process while putting it into practice. The group will become familiar with a method of journaling we call The Oneness Circle Notes. The Oneness Circle Notes form is used in preparation for subsequent Oneness Circle sessions.

Together the group will:

Pause to Meditate Using a Centering Technique.

Review Listening Heartfully.

> As group members interact with one another, there are different forms of communicating. Listening and responding from the heart are powerful forms of communication.

Share a Personal Miracle or Manifestation.

> Using the Oneness Circle Notes form, group members share a personal Miracle or Manifestation.

Discuss Prompts.

> Prompts are defined and examples are given. Group members are encouraged to reflect upon a personal example.

Define and Create Affirmations.

> Affirmations, those powerful tools that assist in manifesting the desires of our heart, are defined and created. The group assists in creating Affirmations together.

Discuss Extending Energy to Others.

> Rather than creating Affirmations for others, a process of extending energy is included.

Prepare for the Third Oneness Circle Meeting.

Close the Oneness Circle Session.

"If you are aware of the guidance from your higher self,
and are receptive to it, that receptivity allows guidance
to flow instantly and immediately."
Gary Zukav

The Third and Subsequent Oneness Circle Meetings

The third meeting, as outlined in Chapter 5, will integrate the concepts and practices from the first two meetings and introduce the Ten Steps of Expressing Affirmations. This format will serve as the structure for future meetings.

Together the group will:

Pause to Meditate Using a Centering Technique.

Share Individual Miracles and Manifestations.

Using the Oneness Circle Notes members take turns sharing personal Miracles and Manifestations.

Share Individual Prompts and Affirmations.

Oneness Circle members take turns sharing Prompts followed by the corresponding Affirmation created to empower each Prompt.

Extend Energy to Others.

Energy is extended to others whose names are listed.

Participate in the Ten Steps of Expressing Affirmations.

The Ten Steps of Expressing Affirmations is an energizing and empowering ritual where each step is read aloud, Affirmations are shared, members listen and respond to each other heartfully, and gratitude is felt and expressed.

As the group participates in the Ten Steps of Expressing Affirmations, steps 9 and 10 serve as a closing to the Oneness Circle session.

Prepare for the Next Oneness Circle Meeting.

"You receive loving guidance and assistance at each moment."
Gary Zukav

The Appendix

The Appendix offers the Oneness Circle members support which includes:

Oneness Circle Invitation Letter.

> A sample letter to invite others to become a member of the Oneness Circle. This letter may be photocopied.

Oneness Circle Contact List.

> A form to gather and distribute contact information for the group members. This form may be photocopied.

Oneness Circle Notes.

> A form used for journaling Miracles, Manifestations, Prompts, and Affirmations. This form may be photocopied.

Sample Affirmations.

> A selection of Affirmations to help inspire members in the creation of Affirmations.

Examples of Compiling Affirmations.

> Two examples of how to compile the individual Affirmations that will be sent to the group.

Glossary.

> A list of definitions of the terminology used throughout the book.

Resources.

> A list of spiritual teachers who have inspired this work and who continue to provide guidance.

Wisdom and Inspiration.

A list of references from which the quotes used throughout the handbook were obtained.

Oneness Circle Notes

Additional copies of the Oneness Circle Notes follow the Appendix.

"You are invited to enter a new arena of creativity and enjoyment
that holds the promise of assisting the transformation
of ourselves and our world."
Barbara Marx Hubbard

PREPARING FOR THE FIRST ONENESS CIRCLE

Ready to create a Oneness Circle? The following steps will guide this process.

1. Invite 2 to 5 people to participate in creating a Oneness Circle.

- For a list of suggested shared aspirations, see page 4.
- A sample Letter of Invitation can be found on page 54.

2. Schedule a date and time for the first meeting.

- Our group currently meets once a month for two hours around a breakfast table.

3. Select a quiet and private location to meet.

- Decide if rotating the location of the meeting month to month allowing each member to share in the hosting responsibility is best for the group, or if renting or using a room at a local facility such as a church or library is best.
- To facilitate confidentially and encourage a community of trust and sharing, include only those who are invited members of the Oneness Circle and recommend that spouses, partners, children, and additional friends or family members not be in attendance.

4. Communicate the date, time, and location to those invited.

5. Gather contact information of each member.

- Collect names, home addresses, phone numbers, and email addresses.
- See the Oneness Circle Contact List form on page 55.

6. Order a copy of the <u>The Oneness Circle Handbook</u> for each participant.

"…you are the eternal possibility, the immeasurable
potential of all that was, is, and will be."
Deepak Chopra

LEADING THE ONENESS CIRCLE

It is recommended that a group facilitator be established to guide the group through the Oneness Circle process for the first three meetings.

The role of the facilitator includes:

- Organizing the group meeting details including inviting group members, scheduling the date, time, and location of each meeting, and organizing materials for the group as discussed in the previous section Preparing for the First Oneness Circle.
- Communicating any information needed such as meeting date, time, and location to group members via email or phone.
- Guiding and directing Oneness Circle members throughout each meeting, and maintaining the structure as outlined at the beginning of each chapter.
- Keeping time by using a timer such as a meditation timer app offered on smartphones to assist the group in following the schedule.

Once the group has completed the first three meetings and has become more familiar with the Oneness Circle process, group members may want to rotate leading and keeping time for the group.

CHAPTER 3

THE FIRST ONENESS CIRCLE MEETING

"Allow your deepest heart's desire for more life,
for higher consciousness, and
greater freedom to express itself fully."
Barbara Marx Hubbard

"Each time you share your own experience it deepens in you.
The word becomes flesh when spoken."
Barbara Marx Hubbard

FACILITATING THE FIRST ONENESS CIRCLE MEETING

The first Oneness Circle meeting introduces the members to the philosophy, practices, and process of the Oneness Circle.

Begin the meeting by giving each member a copy of <u>The Oneness Circle Handbook</u>.

Below is a schedule for the first Oneness Circle meeting based upon a two hour morning session.

8:00	Greet and Meditate - pg. 17 15 minutes	
8:15	Establish Individual and Group Guidance - pgs. 18 - 19 15 minutes	
8:30	Discuss Responding to Life Circumstances - pg. 20 10 minutes	
8:40	Introduce the Oneness Circle Process and Oneness Circle Notes - pgs. 21 - 22 30 minutes	
9:10	Discuss Miracles and Manifestations - pgs. 23 - 25 35 minutes	
9:45	Review Preparing for the Second Oneness Circle Meeting - pg. 26 10 minutes	
9:55	Close the First Oneness Circle Meeting - pg. 27 5 minutes	
10:00	Adjourn	

"Feelings come and go
like clouds in a windy sky.
Conscious breathing
is my anchor."
Thich Nhat Hanh

PAUSING TO MEDITATE USING A CENTERING TECHNIQUE
15 minutes

Begin the Oneness Circle session by relaxing the body, calming the mind, and aligning with the present moment. Set the intention for a focused and supportive meeting.

We offer the following options:

- Lead the group in a guided meditation. Ring a soft bell to bring attention to the present moment. Guide group members with a series of phrases, pausing for a few breaths between each line. For example, "Take a deep breath… quiet the mind… go within… to the essence of being… breathe in awareness… of your true Self… Namasté." Ring the soft bell to bring closure to the meditation.
- Use a soft bell to call the circle to mindfulness. When heard, take a deep breath and follow the sound of the bell, becoming one with it.
- Light a candle mindfully, join hands, and close eyes. Realize stillness, peace, and joy are available in the present moment, bringing us in touch with our true selves.
- Begin a sitting practice with "Let us focus on our breathing, going within to that place of stillness." Sit in silence for a few moments. Conclude with Namasté.
- Listen to an inspirational song. Close the eyes and breathe deeply. Allow the music to wash over you. Listen with your whole body.

"We need safe arenas to test out and experience
the validity of our ideas and to stabilize
our consciousness with others doing the same."
Barbara Marx Hubbard

ESTABLISHING INDIVIDUAL AND GROUP GUIDELINES
15 minutes

The first Oneness Circle is a time to connect with one another, establishing expectations and agreements for individuals and the group as a whole.

Consider the following suggested guidelines:

- Share only personal experiences, keeping anything shared by other members during Oneness Circle confidential.
- Discuss directions or details of the next meeting privately when in a larger group.
- Come prepared with completed Oneness Circle Notes.
- Ask for assistance from the group if needed when completing the Oneness Circle Notes.
- Maintain the Oneness Circle schedule.
- Stay on topic when sharing, avoiding egoic stories of self or others.
- Listen and respond from the heart to Oneness Circle members.
- Support one another in responding to life circumstances.

We suggest each Oneness Circle choose guidelines to foster a supportive environment. As the members of the Oneness Circle agree upon expectations that are important to the group, the guidelines may be recorded and emailed to each member before the next meeting.

Establishing Guidelines for the Group

Using the suggested individual and group guidelines:

1. Each member creates guidelines that are personally important and lists them below. (Allow a few minutes here.)
2. The group facilitator records the guidelines as group members share.

Guidelines that are important to me:

1. _____
    _____
    _____

2. _____
    _____
    _____

3. _____
    _____
    _____

4. _____
    _____
    _____

5. _____
    _____
    _____

6. _____
    _____
    _____

7. _____
    _____
    _____

8. _____
    _____
    _____

"It is not, however, a therapy session.
The circle is a space to experience spiritual intimacy,
non-judgment, unconditional love, and resonance."
Barbara Marx Hubbard

RESPONDING TO LIFE CIRCUMSTANCES
10 minutes

Though the Oneness Circle is not intended to be a therapy group, we do want to recognize that a member may be wrestling with life circumstances that are personal issues, challenges, lessons, dramas, or painful experiences.

We offer the following suggestions:

- Allow each member to discover the answers within themselves, knowing their own mighty soul is guiding them.
- Encourage being gentle with oneself, resisting self-blame.
- Be attuned to the infinite love of the person, remembering you are connected.
- Ask if the group member would like to experience healing touch of the group members by everyone circling the person and touching his or her body as they envision sending love, light, guidance, and appreciation.
- Remember real understanding comes from life experience and from internal guidance.
- Be available to offer resources beyond the group, i.e. pastor, counselor, therapist, help-line, family services.
- Give loving attention and not well-meaning advice.
- Resist pointing out your own experiences and understandings.
- Ask yourself if there are compassionate actions you could do to accompany your loving thoughts.
- Check up or follow up in your own way.
- Remember your mission is not to change anyone other than yourself.

"You will be guided from within."
Rasha

INTRODUCING ONENESS CIRCLE PROCESS AND ONENESS CIRCLE NOTES
30 minutes

As a group, read and review the following sections of the book together to help establish the Oneness Circle philosophy:

- Introduction to <u>The Oneness Circle Handbook</u>, pages XI to XII.
- Inspiration from the members of our founding Oneness Circle, pages XIII to XIV.
- Vision of The Oneness Circle, page 2.
- Purpose of The Oneness Circle, page 3.
- Community of The Oneness Circle, page 4.
- Appendix, pages 53 - 67.
- Oneness Circle Notes, pages 69 - 79.

The Oneness Circle Process

The meeting format we have found successful and recommend includes:

- Pausing to meditate using a centering technique.
- Sharing Miracles and Manifestations.
- Sharing Prompts and a corresponding Affirmation for each Prompt.
- Extending energy to others.
- Participating in the Ten Steps of Expressing Affirmations.
- Preparing for the next Oneness Circle meeting.

"Things that seemed impossible to manifest before
now begin to manifest effortlessly."
Barbara Marx Hubbard

The Oneness Circle Notes

The Oneness Circle Notes is the form for journaling Miracles, Manifestations, Prompts, and Affirmations. This is used by each member to prepare for each Oneness Circle meeting. These notes are used throughout each session. The Oneness Circle Notes consists of:

- Column 1, labeled My Miracles and Manifestations, used to document Miracles and Manifestations experienced since the last Oneness Circle meeting, noting the ones selected to share with Oneness Circle members.
- Column 2, labeled My Prompts, used to document Prompts from Higher Self to share with and hold in the collective energy of the Oneness Circle.
- Column 3, labeled My Affirmations, used to document the Affirmations created based on the Prompts in column 2.
- The bottom box where the first names of people are noted to whom a member wishes to extend energy.

Oneness Circle Notes Date: _____		
My Miracles & Manifestations	**My Prompts**	**My Affirmations**
I extend loving energy to the following people:		

"We are all one manifesting diversely."
Vince Lisi

REFLECTING UPON AND SHARING MIRACLES AND MANIFESTATIONS
35 minutes

Acknowledging our Miracles and Manifestations is important in evolving our Oneness presence. They are the changes and results we experience from listening to our inner guidance and instruction.

Miracles are defined as:

- A change or shift in our perception of self and others.
- Expressions of love with or without observable effects.
- Freedom from fear by living from our Higher Self.
- An expression of inner awareness of Oneness energy.

Examples of a Miracle:

- My joy has been overflowing wherever I am.
- I am listening and responding to more of my inner guidance.
- I became aware of feeling sad, caught myself listening to my ego, and chose again.
- In working with teens experiencing grief, I saw strength and love in each one.
- I am growing in accepting others, choosing again, and seeing the good.
- I was able to see a particular situation from the perspective of my Higher self. As I followed my inner guidance in sending loving energy to my mom, I was able to take a step back, trust Divine order and timing, and release my attachment to outcome. I felt peace.
- More and more of my self-talk has been uplifting.
- I returned to a daily meditation practice.
- I have been letting go of my desired response from another person, and I have been responding with love.

Manifestations are defined as:

- Results we experience from listening to our inner guidance.
- Our co-creations from responding to our Prompts.
- Affirmations that have become true.

Examples of a Manifestation:

- We found the apartment that feels just right.
- I received all the help I needed for my successful project; as it unfolded, I had all the inner strength I needed.
- Downsizing bookshelves was really fun; the task was completed with ease.
- During my partner's surgery of several hours, I found a quiet place to spend my waiting time peacefully.
- I found a yoga class and instructor I enjoy.
- The handout I created for class was easy to read and aesthetically pleasing.
- The condo board met and approved my most recent architectural project.
- A new volunteer opportunity came into my life, and I love it.
- I was able to speak my truth when interviewed, and the magazine article communicates my spirit.
- I found a wonderful sitter for my puppy.

"As you become more comfortable with the process,
you will begin to notice how easily the opportunities flow
and how effortlessly you are able to manifest results
that serve you at the highest level."
Rasha

"Whatever you put your attention on
will grow stronger in your life."
Deepak Chopra

Practice Journaling Miracles and Manifestations

Using the definitions of Miracles and Manifestations on pages 23 and 24:

1. Set a timer for three minutes for the group to reflect upon and record a Miracle or Manifestation experienced recently or over a larger span of time. Record one under the My Miracles and Manifestation column.
2. Go around the circle allowing each member 2 minutes to share a Miracle or Manifestation. Others practice listening heartfully. We suggest giving the timer to the first volunteer. When the timer goes off, it is reset for two minutes before passing it to the next person.

Oneness Circle Notes		
Date: _____		
My Miracles & Manifestations	**My Prompts**	**My Affirmations**
I extend loving energy to the following people:		

PREPARING FOR THE SECOND ONENESS CIRCLE MEETING
10 minutes

At the end of the meeting, take time as a group to review what is needed to prepare for the next Oneness Circle meeting.

Before adjourning select and decide upon:

Host: _____ Date: _____

Time: _____ Location: _____

Home Practice and Preparation:

1. Review the following from The Oneness Circle Handbook.
    *   Introduction, pages XI - XIV.
    *   Chapter 1 - The Oneness Circle, pages 1 - 4.
    *   Chapter 2 - Creation of The Oneness Circle, pages 5 - 14.
    *   Chapter 3 - The First Oneness Circle Meeting, pages 15 - 28.
    *   Appendix, pages 53 - 68.
2. Use the Oneness Circle Notes on page 28.
    *   In the first column journal any Miracles and Manifestations as they occur between now and the next session. This practice helps members remember and choose Miracles and Manifestations to bring to the Oneness Circle. Journaling also assists in acknowledging and expressing gratitude for the Miracles and Manifestations.
    *   The Prompt and Affirmation columns are not used at this time. These will be addressed at the next Oneness Circle meeting.
3. Prepare the Oneness Circle Notes one or two days before the next Oneness Circle meeting. This preparation assists in contributing to an inspiring meeting.
    *   Review the Miracles and Manifestations journaled in the Oneness Circle Notes. Choose one to share with the group.
4. Send an email if hosting the next meeting, reminding members of the date, time, and location of the next meeting.
5. Respond to the host's email.

Compile and send a copy of the agreed upon group guidelines to each member.

"For, the power of Love is quite literally unstoppable,
exercising its capability to manifest fully and to create itself –
its vibrational essence - in every conceivable expression of life."
Rasha

CLOSING THE FIRST ONENESS CIRCLE MEETING
5 minutes

When it is time to adjourn the meeting, we suggest taking a couple minutes to gather within a circle for closure.

The following is a suggested closing for the first Oneness Circle.

- Gather in a circle, closing the eyes, focusing on the breath, going within.
- Shift the focus of your attention to feeling the breath within your heart center.
- Inhale and exhale from this area five or six times.
- Call to mind something you are grateful for that occurred during the Oneness Circle meeting; feel the love, appreciation, gratitude, and/or compassion that accompanies this thought.
- Complete the closing by silently acknowledging and thanking each member of the Oneness Circle, perhaps with a bow or a Namasté.

Oneness Circle Notes

Form for Home Practice to Prepare for Session Two

My Miracles & Manifestations	My Prompts	My Affirmations

I extend loving energy to the following people:

THE SECOND ONENESS CIRCLE MEETING

"When you permit yourself the luxury of openly, unabashedly,
fantasizing about what it is you truly yearn for, and dream of,
you set into motion the energetic parameters
for manifesting your heart's desire."
Rasha

"And allow the circumstances that present themselves
to nudge you in the direction of your highest possible good."
Rasha

FACILITATING THE SECOND ONENESS CIRCLE MEETING

During the second Oneness Circle meeting, the members will continue the process that began in session one and practice the next steps of the Oneness Circle.

Below is a structure for the second Oneness Circle meeting based on a two hour morning session.

8:00	Greet and Meditate - pg. 17	15 minutes
8:15	Discuss Listening Heartfully - pg. 31	10 minutes
8:25	Share a Miracle or Manifestation - pg. 31	10 minutes
8:35	Discuss Prompts - pgs. 32 - 33	30 minutes
9:05	Define and Create Affirmations - pgs. 34 - 37	35 minutes
9:40	Discuss Extending Energy to Others - pg. 38	10 minutes
9:50	Review Preparing for the Third Oneness Circle Meeting - pg. 40	5 minutes
9:55	Close the Second Oneness Circle Meeting - pg. 40	5 minutes
10:00	Adjourn	

"Be aware of your loving intentions, and be sure that
you are not undermining the progress of another by preempting
this process of integration with well-meaning advice."
Rasha

LISTENING HEARTFULLY
10 minutes

Our listening heartfully to each other is one of the most loving gifts we give another.

We offer the following suggestions:

- Relax your shoulders, take a deep breath, smile, feel the warm glow and love within.
- Feel connected as you remember you are one with the person sharing, one with each other, and one with Oneness energy and all that is.
- Convey nonverbally you are interested, giving eye contact as you show you care.
- Give appropriate silence.
- Feel the essence of the content conveyed.
- Look for feelings behind words as you pay attention to body language and tone of voice. Emotions being expressed are sometimes more important than what is said.
- Ignore the clamor of your mind with its thoughts of Oh, I also…, I've been there…, I did that…, I think you just need to….
- Avoid motions that might be distracting such as being fidgety, drumming fingers, crossing arms, or sneaking glances at watch or timer.

SHARING A MIRACLE OR MANIFESTATION
10 minutes

Using the Oneness Circle Notes home practice form on page 28, share one Miracle or Manifestation.

Using the timer, allow each member one minute to share while others practice listening heartfully.

"We know that every prompting of the spirit
will be empowered by the spirit within us to accomplish it."
Vince Lisi

IDENTIFYING PROMPTS
30 minutes

A nudge, idea, or cue that arises from our inner guidance, our intuition, giving us direction is what we call a Prompt. This guidance comes from the Higher Self as we connect to the present moment.

This inner guidance can be experienced, heard, and felt through our heart, mind, feelings, and/or body sensations as we align and merge with the Divine, our Source that is within.

Listening to our Prompts is helpful in expressing our true self and manifesting our purpose. Through the practice of listening to our inner voice, we begin to hear the guidance more clearly and have more and more confidence in following our Prompts.

One way we can experience our inner guidance is aligning with the present moment by relaxing the body and quieting the mind using a focused breathing meditation technique.

Examples of Prompts from our inner guidance:

- Remember my spiritual principles in the selling of our house.
- Be patient and see the Higher Self in all others.
- Plan a celebration for all the helpers involved.
- Send loving energy to my cousin.
- Visit my friend in skilled nursing, taking a small gift.
- Open to the meaning behind this experience.

"Ideas that come from your head are different
than prompts that come from the heart, the inner self."
Vince Lisi

"You must be willing to hear what your
intuition says and to act accordingly."
Gary Zukav

Practice Identifying Prompts

Using the definitions of Prompts on page 32:

1. Set a timer for three minutes for members to reflect upon and record a Prompt experienced
    in the past. Record this under the My Prompts column of the Oneness Circle notes.
*   Go around the circle allowing each member two minutes to share one Prompt while others
    practice listening heartfully. We suggest giving the timer to the first volunteer. When the
    timer goes off, it is reset for two minutes before passing it to the next person.

Oneness Circle Notes		
Date: _____		
My Miracles & Manifestations	**My Prompts**	**My Affirmations**
I extend loving energy to the following people:		

"They are like seeds planted in soil."
Louise Hay

DEFINING AND CREATING AFFIRMATIONS
35 minutes

Affirmations, what we express to ourselves and others, are a powerful tool in helping us manifest the desires and dreams of our hearts. They assist us in feeling the inspiration and guidance from following the direction of our inner wisdom.

An Affirmation is created after identifying a Prompt. Affirmations may be general or specific in content. As we create and use Affirmations, a sense of confidence is built. We learn to trust that we are given the support and guidance we need.

Affirmations:

- Focus on our individual expressions, and are about us rather than the events and life circumstances of another.
- Facilitate the beginning points of change bringing Prompts to form, though not all Prompts need an Affirmation.
- Lead the way in assisting us to manifest our Prompts by assisting us in setting an inspired intention, opening us to our next guided steps.
- Help us consciously create a meaningful life by empowering, reinforcing, and nourishing our Prompts.

In creating an Affirmation, it is important to:

- Express desires through positive words. Positive words combined with a feeling of gratitude assist us in feeling and knowing the power of our Oneness energy.
    Instead of: My depression about my flu is gone.
    Affirm: I give my body the rest, nourishment, and care it needs.
- Use the present tense.
    Instead of: I need money to pay my bills.
    Affirm: I responsibly manage the money that comes my way.
- Go beyond the circumstances of the present moment and express the Affirmation as if it were already true.
    Instead of: Someday I hope to have supportive people in my life.
    Affirm: I love the supportive people in my life who are helping me grow spiritually.

"It is easy for me to reprogram the computer of my mind.
All of life is change, and my mind is ever new."
Louise Hay

The following are examples of Affirmations and corresponding Prompts:

For the Prompt: Remember my spiritual principle in the selling of our house.

Affirm: The selling of our house is in Divine order. The more I love and embrace change, the more my life unfolds easily and effortlessly. I trust that my changes are part of my evolutionary process.

For the Prompt: Be patient and see the Higher Self in all others.

Affirm: I see myself as the Source, God, created me and sees me, and that is how I relate to the world. As I interact with others I remember the line from A Course in Miracles Workbook, "The light in you is all that I see."

For the Prompt: Plan a celebration for all the helpers involved.

Affirm: I am so thankful for the tag sale help I received from friends. As I express from spirit and pure joy, a fun and loving celebration unfolds easily.

For the Prompt: Send loving energy to my cousin.

Affirm: I am soul guided as to where and when to extend to my cousin. I see him with acceptance and love. I have no connection to outcomes.

For the Prompt: Visit my friend in skilled nursing, taking a small gift.

Affirm: This month I find time for my loving, giving visit with my friend. As I bring Oneness and presence, joy and renewed connections are experienced.

For the Prompt: Open to the meaning behind this experience.

Affirm: I open myself to discover the meaning behind the situation.

Sometimes help is needed in creating an Affirmation regarding a certain Prompt. We suggest asking for assistance from members of the Oneness Circle. See sample Affirmations on pages 57 and 58.

Additional Thoughts about Affirmations

As we incorporate Affirmations in our lives, it is important to know that they are created with Divine order in mind. As we affirm, we release any attachment to outcome, allow the details to unfold without resistance, and surrender to the timing of the universe. We trust that we are guided and have what we need.

"You cannot stand in resistance of them and receive them at the same time."
Esther and Jerry Hicks

"…you plant your intention in the womb of creation
and allow the universe to orchestrate the details."
Deepak Chopra

Practice Creating Affirmations

Using the examples of Prompts and Affirmations on page 35:

1. Set a timer for three minutes for the group to reflect upon and record an Affirmation for the Prompt below.
2. Ask group members to practice creating an Affirmation together. Allow time for group discussion of the construction of the Affirmations, keeping in mind to use positive words. Create a statement in the present tense as if it were already true.
• Record this Affirmation under the My Affirmations column. For example, I find the right time to make a delicious and healthy meal for my friend; I extend love and joy as it is delivered.

Oneness Circle Notes		
Date: _____		
My Miracles & Manifestations	**My Prompts**	**My Affirmations**
I extend loving energy to the following people:		

"Affirmations are principally about oneself.
We can extend energy to others and create energy fields
that are helpful to others, but each other must be receptive
so that this energy might be effective."
Vince Lisi

EXTENDING ENERGY TO OTHERS
10 minutes

When we construct Affirmations, they are about our own personal Prompts based on our inner guidance. While we may want to intend a specific outcome for our friends and/or family, it is best that we focus our attention on our journey rather than trying to decide what may be best for another person's life path. In acknowledging that we are each on our own unique journey, we are able to shift our focus to honor the Oneness energy within each other.

Rather than creating Affirmations for others, we have incorporated a way to include them in a positive, loving, and non-judgmental way by extending loving energy.

The box at the bottom of Oneness Circle Notes may be used to list the names of people to whom members wish to extend energy.

We offer the following suggestions:

- It is important to mention first names without telling stories about the people or the reasons the names have been listed.
- It is not necessary to have knowledge of the details surrounding a person.
- There is no need to share the current circumstances or wishes for a desired outcome.
- Leaving out the details keeps the group energy on a higher level by allowing the Oneness energy to guide and direct.

"Simply remember the bliss,
and the needle of your attention swings immediately toward it.
Instead of focusing on a problem or pain,
concentrate on bliss and joy."
Barbara Marx Hubbard

"Look fondly on the world.
Generate Oneness, not separation or fear.
Serve the inner connectedness with all each day."
Vince Lisi

Practice Extending Energy

Using the guidelines for Extending Energy to Others on page 38:

1. Set a timer for two minutes for the group to reflect upon and record first names of people to whom they feel moved to send loving energy. Ask members to list the names in the bottom box of the Oneness Circle Notes.

•   Go around the circle as each member shares the first names of others. For example, I extend loving energy to David and Linda. Hold these people in the collective energy of the group. Remember to use first names only and not to add any explanation or story as to why loving energy is being sent.

Oneness Circle Notes		
Date: _____		
My Miracles & Manifestations	**My Prompts**	**My Affirmations**
I extend loving energy to the following people:		

PREPARING FOR THE THIRD
ONENESS CIRCLE MEETING
5 minutes

Before adjourning select and decide upon:

Host: _____ Date: _____

Time: _____ Location: _____

Home Practice and Preparation:

1. Review the following from <u>The Oneness Circle Handbook</u>.
   - Chapter 4 - The Second Oneness Circle Meeting, pages 29 - 41.
2. Use the Oneness Circle Notes on page 41:
   - In the first column journal Miracles and Manifestations as they occur between now and the next session.
   - In the second column record some of the Prompts received. Prompts can be communicated in a variety of ways. It may be helpful to set aside a period of quiet reflection and/or meditation to assist with identifying Prompts.
3. Prepare the Oneness Circle Notes one or two days before the next Oneness Circle meeting.
   - Review the Miracles and Manifestations journaled in the Oneness Circle Notes. Choose one to share with the group.
   - Review the Prompts recorded in the second column. Select one to bring to the collective energy of the group. Write the corresponding Affirmation for the Prompt in the third column.
4. Send an email if hosting the next meeting, reminding members of the date, time, and location of the next meeting.
5. Respond to the host's email.

CLOSING THE SECOND ONENESS CIRCLE MEETING
5 minutes

Close the Oneness Circle. See the suggested closing found on page 27.

Oneness Circle Notes

Form for Home Practice to Prepare for Session Two

My Miracles & Manifestations	My Prompts	My Affirmations

I extend loving energy to the following people:

THE THIRD AND SUBSEQUENT ONENESS CIRCLE MEETINGS

"We become mirrors in which others can
see the "glory" of who they truly are.
By holding a clear surface for others to see themselves
as we see them, we mature ourselves..."
Barbara Marx Hubbard

"Resonance means responding, echoing back
and affirming the highest in one another.
It occurs when our hearts are open and we share deeply
from our essential selves in an environment of
safety and non-judgment."
Barbara Marx Hubbard

FACILITATING THE THIRD AND SUBSEQUENT ONENESS CIRCLE MEETINGS

The third Oneness Circle meeting integrates all of the concepts and practices that were explored during the first two meetings and follows the standard format of a typical Oneness Circle.

Below is a structure for the third and subsequent Oneness Circle meetings based on a two hour morning session.

8:00　Greet and Meditate - pg. 17
15 minutes

8:15　Share Miracles and Manifestation - pg. 45
35 minutes

8:50　Share Prompts, Affirmations, and Exend Loving Energy - pg. 45
35 minutes

9:25　Participate in the Ten Steps of Expressing Affirmations - pgs. 46 - 49
30 minutes

9:55　Review Preparing for the Next Oneness Circle Meeting - pg. 50
5 minutes

10:00　Adjourn

"If you choose to focus your attention on the strengths of others,
on the virtues of others, on that part of others that strives for the highest,
you run through your system the higher-frequency
currents of appreciation, acceptance and love.
Your energy and influence radiate instantaneously from soul to soul.
You become an effective instrument of constructive change."
Gary Zukav

"And respect the magnificence of the processes of the beings who journey by your side,
by allowing for the full expression of their humanness - and your own."
Rasha

SHARING MIRACLES AND MANIFESTATIONS
35 minutes

Sharing some of the Miracles and Manifestations that have occurred since the last meeting offers a time of much joy and inspiration. Refer to pages 23 and 24 for definitions of Miracles and Manifestations if needed.

Set a timer for five minutes for a volunteer to share the Miracles and Manifestations from his or her Oneness Circle Notes as members listen heartfully. Suggestions for listening heartfully are offered on page 31. While listening, maintain the focus of your loving attention on the person sharing, without any interruption.

When the timer goes off, the member finishes sharing, resets the timer for five minutes, and passes it to the next person on the left.

Option: This transition from one member to another offers an opportunity to chant Om or ring a soft bell to refocus on heartful listening.

SHARING PROMPTS, AFFIRMATIONS, AND EXTENDING ENERGY TO OTHERS
35 minutes

Sharing Prompts, the guidance that arises from inner wisdom, followed by an Affirmation for each Prompt, help us consciously co-create a life guided by Oneness energy.

Set a timer for five minutes for the first member volunteer to share Prompts and an Affirmation for each Prompt from the member's Oneness Circle Notes. Members listen heartfully. (These Affirmations will be shared again during the Ten Steps of Expressing Affirmations.)

After Prompts and Affirmations are shared, names of people to whom the member would like to extend loving energy are stated. For example: I extend loving energy to _____.

When the timer goes off, the member finishes sharing, resets the timer for 5 minutes, and passes it to the next person on the left.

Option: This transition from one member to another offers an opportunity to chant Om or ring a soft bell to refocus on heartful listening.

"This environment of resonance is created in circles
with processes of attunement, deep sharing,
attention to the heart, and
non-judgment of one another."
Barbara Marx Hubbard

PARTICIPATING IN THE TEN STEPS OF EXPRESSING AFFIRMATIONS
30 minutes

The Ten Steps of Expressing Affirmations is a sequence of universal principles read together as a way of affirming and honoring the highest and best within ourselves and one another. When shared as a group, it assists in building a collective field of supportive energy. As we experience this process, we are reminded that Divine energy is here, now and always.

Participating in the Ten Steps of Expressing Affirmations allows us to jointly express the desires of our hearts and empowers us collectively to co-create and participate in the unfolding of our life path as we are guided by Oneness energy. As a result, we express wonder, joy, and gratitude as we acknowledge and experience our connection to Oneness.

The Ten Steps of Expressing Affirmations sequence is found on page 49. The following is an outline to guide the group through the process of these steps.

Steps 1 through 6

Members take turns reading steps 1 through 6 aloud, with the group in unison reading the bold print words at the end of each step. While reading, feel the truth, power, and energy behind each statement.

Step 7

In preparing for the sharing of Affirmations, all group members read step 7 in unison.

Following the reading of step 7, group members pause momentarily to go within. Aligning the mind and body with the present moment, assists in members sharing and responding from their highest and best selves. We offer the following centering technique: Close the eyes and take a few deep breaths. Allow the mind and body to settle into this moment and allow the heart to open.

After the centering practice, members begin sharing their Affirmations.

Sharing of Affirmations

Members listen with open hearts to all Affirmations, and then take turns echoing back the essence of each one shared. This experience of responding from Higher Self to Higher Self, sometimes even repeating the exact words, is a moving experience for both the giver, the receiver, and all who are present.

To begin, the first member sharing his or her affirmations chooses who will be responding to each affirmation they have recorded on the Oneness Circle Notes, allowing each listener to respond once. When a member has one affirmation, all listening members will have an opportunity to respond.

Once the affirmations have been assigned, the first member shares his or her first Affirmation. As the Affirmation is read, other group members listen heartfully as they align with the present moment and to his or her Higher Self. As any thoughts or urges to speak rise up while listening, it is helpful to return attention to the present moment and the person who is sharing by focusing on the breath.

After the Affirmation is read, the group members pause and connect with his or her breath, allowing a moment to go within. The designated member responds to the Affirmation succinctly by echoing back the essence of the Affirmation, guided by his or her Higher Self. Each response is one to three sentences and mirrors back what was shared without extra commentary or well-meaning advice. We offer the following example:

> Affirmation: I am soul guided as to where and when to extend to my friend. I see him with acceptance and love. I have no attachment to outcomes.
>
> Response: I see you listening and responding to your friend. You are guided as to when to talk to your friend, and you are guided what to say. Love and presence go with you, filling you with confidence and joy.

Members acknowledge and embrace partnering with Oneness energy and honoring the Highest Self in one another by lovingly listening with open hearts and echoing back the essence of each Affirmation, rather than a personal story, advice, or self-reference. It is important to not add any personal interpretation of another's life path. We offer the following suggestions of what to avoid when responding from the heart:

> Personal Story - Oh, that happened to me before…
> Advice - It may be helpful if you try….
> Self-Reference - I remember one time…

This response process is repeated for each Affirmation for the first group member. After all of one member's Affirmations have received a response, another member follows this same process of sharing each of his or her Affirmations followed by heartful responses from group members. The transition from one member to another again offers an opportunity to chant Om or ring a soft bell to refocus.

Step 8

After all Oneness Circle members are finished sharing and responding to the Affirmations of each member, step 8 is read in unison.

In this step, gratitude is expressed for all Miracles and Manifestations of the Affirmations, knowing each member is guided and has what is needed.

As members allow the Oneness to guide, any attachment to outcome is released as life unfolds in Divine order.

Expression of Wonder, Joy, and Gratitude

Next, members stand and physically express the wonder, joy, and gratitude coming from feeling and knowing each Affirmation has been manifested. Dance or move around the room before joining in a circle holding hands, and pausing to go within.

Steps 9 and 10

Oneness Circle members read steps 9 and 10 in unison as a closing, feeling connection to the Oneness energy, to each other, and to all that is.

> "Currents of joy, fields of bliss lift the vibrational field within you."
> Barbara Marx Hubbard

TEN STEPS OF EXPRESSING AFFIRMATIONS

1. I am connected with Oneness energy. I go within, allowing the Light to embrace me. **I am connected.**

2. I feel my connection to the Oneness energy within me. I see this Light in all others, and I know that we are all connected to each other and to the Source. **I feel my connection.**

3. I listen and respond to inner guidance. I allow my energy to flow creatively, lovingly, and powerfully. My life evolves in accordance with Oneness energy. **I listen and respond.**

4. I am guided and directed as I co-create with Oneness energy, remembering who I truly am. **I am guided and directed.**

5. I trust in Oneness energy knowing that everything is unfolding in Divine order for the highest good. **I trust in Oneness energy.**

6. I release all attachment to outcome allowing the Oneness energy to guide me. **I release all attachment to outcome.**

7. **I now share my affirmations with my partners, knowing I am consciously co-creating a joyous, peaceful life, filled with the desires of my heart. I now share my affirmations.**

We share our affirmations,
listening and responding to each other
from the heart.

8. **I express gratitude knowing that I have each desire of my heart.**

Allow 68 seconds or more to physically express
this wonder, joy, and gratitude.

"Within 17 seconds of focusing on something, a matching vibration becomes activated."
"And if you manage to stay purely focused upon any thought for as little as 68 seconds, the vibration is powerful enough that its manifestation begins."
Esther and Jerry Hicks

9. **I feel the magnificence of who I am. My journey is a glorious adventure. I choose to accept the highest and best in me.**

10. **I radiate joy, peace, and bliss of my connection to Oneness. All is well. Namasté.**

PREPARING FOR THE NEXT AND SUBSEQUENT ONENESS CIRCLE MEETINGS
5 minutes

Before adjourning select and decide upon:

Host: _____ Date: _____
Time: _____ Location: _____

Organize the process of compiling and sending individual Affirmations for the group:

> Select a Oneness Circle member who will compile and send the individual Affirmations to all members. The host of the current meeting could accept this responsibility. Or another member could volunteer.

> Member to compile Affirmations: _____

> Select a date for the individual Affirmations to be emailed to the member who is organizing the list. If meeting monthly, it is helpful to request Affirmations be sent three or four days following the meeting.

> Due date for Affirmations to be sent: _____

Home Practice and Preparation:

1. Send the Affirmations personally shared at the meeting to the group member who will compile them. He or she will compile the Affirmations and then send the list to all members. See pages 59 and 60 for examples of how to organize Affirmations for the group.
2. Review personal Affirmations as part of a daily spiritual practice, feeling and knowing that each one has been manifested. Affirmations assist in aligning what we think, say, and feel. In reviewing Affirmations, we offer the following suggestions:
   * Take whatever action is inspired.
   * Release any attachment to outcome.
   * Allow the details to unfold without resistance.
   * Surrender to the timing of the universe.
   * Trust, trust, trust!!!
3. Review the following from The Oneness Circle Handbook.
   * Chapter 5 - The Third and Subsequent Oneness Circle Meetings, pages 43 - 52.

4. Use the Oneness Circle Notes on page 52:
   - In the first column journal Miracles and Manifestations as they occur between now and the next session.
   - In the second column record some of the Prompts received.
5. Prepare the Oneness Circle Notes one or two days before the next Oneness Circle meeting.
   - Review the Miracles and Manifestations journaled in the Oneness Circle Notes. Choose a few to share with the group. In planning which Miracles and Manifestations to share, keep in mind that each member will be given approximately five minutes.
   - Review the Prompts recorded in the second column. Select a few to bring to the collective energy of the group. Write the corresponding Affirmation for each Prompt in the third column.
   - In the bottom box list the first names of friends or family members to whom loving energy will be extended.
6. Send an email if hosting the next meeting, reminding members of the date, time, and location of the next meeting.
7. Respond to the host's email.

Additional Oneness Circle Notes for subsequent Oneness Circle meetings can be found following the appendix on pages 69 - 79.

"Select your own affirmations,
use them in your meditative time in the Inner Sanctuary,
and repeat them throughout the day.
Whenever your thoughts veer downward toward an old problem,
worrying a wound aimlessly, consciously shift your attention to the affirmation.
Let the affirmations become your mantras and
experience incarnating these qualities in your being."
Barbara Marx Hubbard

Oneness Circle Notes

Date: _____

My Miracles & Manifestations	My Prompts	My Affirmations

I extend loving energy to the following people:

SUPPORT FOR ONENESS CIRCLE MEMBERS

"What I can imagine, the Universe can deliver."
Esther and Jerry Hicks

LETTER OF INVITATION

Dear Friend:

I am interested in building a community of like-minded individuals who are dedicated to evolving their personal spiritual growth.

I have found a process that can assist me in creating this environment, and I am inviting you to join me.

Co-authors Carol Stanley and Stacie Will participated in a group process they call **The Oneness Circle**. They were so inspired by their personal growth and group connection that they wrote a handbook to assist others in building their own Oneness Circle family. The book is titled **The Oneness Circle Handbook: A Guide for Evolving Spiritual Growth in a Supportive and Structured Group Environment.**

The following is an excerpt from the introduction of The Oneness Circle Handbook to give you a taste of what is being offered:

> *"The Oneness Circle is a structured meeting of people who want to evolve their spiritual growth in a supportive environment of shared information and inspiration.*
>
> *"We believe there is great wisdom within all of us. This wisdom expresses itself in the form of Prompts, those individual expressions that come from our inner being. As we go within aligning our mind, body, and heart within the present moment, we allow the flow of this guidance and direction.*
>
> *"It is through this practice of listening to our inner voice and allowing it to blossom into expression that our inner guidance flows creatively, lovingly, and powerfully. As we join with other like-minded individuals, we gain confidence in our ability to hear the wisdom within and follow its direction."*
>
> *- Carol Stanley & Stacie Will, The Oneness Circle Handbook.*

Meetings are typically once per month, last two hours, and consist of 3 to 6 people. The Oneness Circle Handbook will guide us step by step through this process of building our Oneness Circle.

Together, we can create a community where we have the opportunity to explore and grow in our understanding of living from our truest, Highest Self.

I will be contacting you soon with details of the first Oneness Circle meeting.

Yours in Oneness,

ONENESS CIRCLE CONTACT LIST

Name	
Address	
Email	
Home Phone	
Cell Phone	
Name	
Address	
Email	
Home Phone	
Cell Phone	
Name	
Address	
Email	
Home Phone	
Cell Phone	
Name	
Address	
Email	
Home Phone	
Cell Phone	
Name	
Address	
Email	
Home Phone	
Cell Phone	
Name	
Address	
Email	
Home Phone	
Cell Phone	

Oneness Circle Notes

Date: _____

My Miracles & Manifestations	My Prompts	My Affirmations

I extend loving energy to the following people:

SAMPLE AFFIRMATIONS

Acceptance of others

- My heart is filled to overflowing with feelings of love and acceptance.
- "The light in you is all that I see." - A Course in Miracles Workbook
- As I honor each mighty soul with heartfelt and soulful attention, I listen and respond from the heart.
- I see each and every person with whom I interact as a mighty soul.

Change

- The more I embrace change, the more my life unfolds.
- I trust that all my changes are part of my evolutionary process.
- The timing of these events is coordinated, so that the upcoming transition is made with comfort, ease, excitement, fun, and gratitude.
- I live without fear. I notice when I am out of alignment and choose again.

Communication

- I communicate with ease as I speak from the heart.

Finances

- All the resources we need for each step of our life change is provided.
- I have everything I need at this moment.
- I hook into pure joy and watch everything unfold. I relax into this knowing.

Gratitude

- I find the feeling place of appreciation.
- I rejoice in the abundant blessings in my life.
- My joy radiates throughout my body.
- I am thankful for all the good in my life.
- My heart is light and my life is joy filled.

Guidance

- I listen and pay close attention to my gentle cues.
- I know that when I am guided, I am empowered.
- I listen very closely to my Higher Self as it guides me to materials, content, and people on my enlightenment path.
- I recognize my inner guide is there with the guidance, wisdom, and love I need in creating my life experience.

- I silence the ego when searching for an answer, and I listen.
- I listen, respond, co-create, and evolve my soul.

Health

- I release the need for anything that does not support me.
- My body communicates its needs to me, and I lovingly listen and attend to its direction.
- I treat my body with love and respect.

Past

- I move beyond limiting beliefs and allow myself to express freely and creatively.
- As I release what has been, I remove its power over the present.
- I let go of that which blocks my creativity, growth, and love.
- I am aware that when I am out of alignment, I freely and willingly choose again. I am at peace.

Projects

- Each project I take on is completed with wisdom, love, and ease.
- My class lessons are inspiring, helpful, and fun.
- I live in the present moment. This is my point of strength and creation.

Relationships

- I am grateful for the supportive people in my life who are helping me grow spiritually.
- My relationship with my partner continues to grow authentically.
- I find the right time to talk to my friend.

Travel

- Our travel is fun and full of love and connections.
- I live boldly. I travel with grace and ease.

ONENESS CIRCLE GROUP AFFIRMATIONS
Meeting Date
(EXAMPLE #1)

Member Name

- My heart is filled to overflowing with feelings of love and acceptance.

Member Name

- I live without fear. I notice when I am out of alignment and choose again.
- As I honor each mighty soul with heartfelt and soulful attention, I listen and respond from the heart.
- I know when I am guided, I am empowered.

Member Name

- I communicate with ease as I speak from the heart.
- I move beyond limiting beliefs and allow myself to express freely and creatively.

Member Name

- I find the feeling place of appreciation.

Member Name

- I release the need for anything that does not support me.
- I have everything I need at this moment.

Member Name

- I live in the present moment. This is my point of strength and creation.

ONENESS CIRCLE GROUP AFFIRMATIONS
Meeting Date
(EXAMPLE #1)

Member Name	My heart is filled to overflowing with feelings of love and acceptance.
Member Name	I live without fear. I notice when I am out of alignment and choose again. As I honor each mighty soul with heartfelt and soulful attention, I listen and respond from the heart. I know when I am guided, I am empowered.
Member Name	I communicate with ease as I speak from the heart. I move beyond limiting beliefs and allow myself to express freely and creatively.
Member Name	I find the feeling place of appreciation.
Member Name	I release the need for anything that does not support me. I have everything I need at this moment.
Member Name	I live in the present moment. This is my point of strength and creation.

GLOSSARY

Affirmation: A strong verbal expression of an inner guidance Prompt from the Higher Self, stated in positive words in the present tense.

Awareness: A felt knowingness of our connection and unity to the Oneness energy and to all its expressions.

Co-create: To focus creative energy and manifest one's inner wisdom by following the Prompts from Higher Self.

Consciousness: Self-awareness that may be of the mind or of the soul.

Divine Order: A keen awareness of the Higher Self and its connection to Source. The knowing that we are exactly where we need to be in this moment and that everything is unfolding for the highest good.

Ego: Self-identification with the mind, emotions, physical body, and life circumstances. Ego sees comparatively and competitively, seeking things that will not fulfill on a spiritual level. It gives way to fear, jealousy, attack thoughts, littleness, arrogance, etc. It is also known as the little me.

Energy: A connecting and guiding force that is present in all things.

> "The electrical current at the basis of everything that exists."
> – Esther and Jerry Hicks

Evolve: Our growth and expansion of our sense of Oneness energy through our Higher Self.

> "Spirit is always moving us to its greater expansion."
> – Vince Lisi

Heart: The center point of our Higher Self.

Higher Self: That loving, guiding, all-knowing part of us that exists in the nonphysical dimension. It is the Source energy that is within us all. It is our soul, our inner being. It is my true self that knows I am what God is doing on earth. It is also known as the Big Me.

Intention: The willingness to carry out an idea or inspiration, accompanied by the confidence that it is obtainable.

Intuition: An inner knowing often expressed and experienced through feelings rather than words.

> "A knowing that arises in you before thinking."
> – Vince Lisi

> "…perception beyond the physical senses that is meant to assist you."
> – Gary Zukav

Life Force: The energy experienced as our breath and awareness. It is the Source energy within us that enlivens us.

> "Stream of well-being, the eternally expanding vibrational stream from which all things flow."
> – Esther and Jerry Hicks

Light: The Divine inspiration and intelligence experienced through our consciousness and awareness.

Manifestation: A result brought into the physical world created by following inner guidance, sometimes with the help of an Affirmation.

Meditation: The state of quieting the mind, relaxing the body, and going within to that inner place that is formless and often called Higher Self, heart, or soul.

Miracle: A change in our perception, seeing things from the perspective of the Higher Self as we shift from our identification with ego.

Namasté: The light within me honors the light within you. The soul/spirit within me sees the soul/spirit within you. The God/Goddess within me recognizes and honors the God/Goddess within you. When spoken to another person, it is commonly accompanied by a slight bow made with hands pressed together, palms touching and fingers pointed upwards in front of the chest.

Oneness: An awareness and knowing that we are connected to each other, to all that is, and to the Source.

Oneness Circle: A meeting of a group of individuals who desire to understand and experience Oneness energy within. They gather regularly to share Miracles, Manifestations, Prompts, and Affirmations as they connect Higher Self to Higher Self.

Oneness Energy: The resonance that we experience when we feel the connection to each other, to all that is, to Source, to God.

Presence: Soul awareness of the Divine within.

Persona: The mind, emotions, physical body, and life circumstances through which the Higher Self co-creates and manifests on earth.

Prompt: The nudge, idea, or cue from our inner guidance giving Divine direction.

Resonance: The vibration, vitalizing spirit, or emotional atmosphere experienced when we feel our connection with Oneness energy.

> "The response of harmony or discord of all things to all things."
> – Esther and Jerry Hicks

Soul: The part of us that is our Higher Self. Also referred to as our spirit or Essential Self.

> "It is a positive, purposeful force at the core of your being. It is that part of you that understands the impersonal nature of the energy dynamics in which you are involved, that loves without restriction and accepts without judgment."
> – Gary Zukav

Source: The eternally-expanding higher vibrational energy in which we participate. It is the guiding force of evolution.

Spiritual Practice: Experiences such as meditation, prayer, focused breathing, yoga, qigong, tai chi, study, service, being in nature, music, dance, and/or chanting which remind us of our connection to Oneness energy. This energy can radiate through our persona.

Universal Principles: Truths common to all.

Vibration: See Resonance.

RESOURCES

Books

A Course in Miracles - Foundation for Inner Peace
A New Earth - Eckhart Tolle
Emergence - Barbara Marx Hubbard
I Can Do It! - Louise Hay
Oneness - Rasha
Seat of the Soul - Gary Zukav
The Power of Now - Eckhart Tolle
The Seven Spiritual Laws of Success - Deepak Chopra

Websites

Louise Hay
http://www.louisehay.com/
http://www.louisehay.com/affirmations/
The Chopra Center - Deepak Chopra
http://www.chopra.com/
http://www.chopra.com/ccl/sections/meditation
http://www.chopra.com/ccl/guided-meditations
The Teachings of Abraham (Esther and Jerry Hicks)
http://www.abraham-hicks.com/
Vince Lisi
http://www.nowcreations.org/

WISDOM AND INSPIRATION

Introduction

Lisi, Vince, Enlightenment Class, December 19, 2012.

Tolle, Eckhart, <u>A New Earth</u>, (Plume, a member of Penguin Group (USA) Inc., 2006), p. 139.

Tyson, Neil de Grasse, Cosmos, Episode One, March 9, 2014.

Chapter One

<u>Holy Bible</u>, Revised Standard Version, Thomas Nelson & Sons, 1953, Matthew 18:20.

Hubbarb, Barbara Marx, <u>Emergence, the Shift from Ego to Essence</u>, (Hampton Roads Publishing Company, Inc., 2001), p. 71, 75, 191, 192.

Lisi, Vince, The Light Group: Vision, Purpose, Guide CD, June 2011.

Rasha, <u>Oneness</u>, (Earthstar Press, 2003), p. 17.

Thich Nhat Hanh, A Talk with Oprah Winfrey, May 12, 2013, OWN Network.

Chapter Two

Chopra, Deepak, <u>The Seven Spiritual Laws of Success,</u> (Amber-Allen Publishing, Inc., 1994) p. 10.

Hubbard, Barbara Marx, <u>Emergence, the Shift from Ego to Essence</u>, (Hampton Roads Publishing Company, Inc., 2001), p. 76, 153.

Rasha, <u>Oneness</u>, (Earthstar Press, 20003), p. 22.

Zukav, Gary, <u>Seat of the Soul</u>, (Fireside, Simon and Schuster, 1990), p. 31, 80, 101, 128, 202.

Chapter Three

Chopra, Deepak, <u>The Seven Spiritual Laws of Success</u>, (Amber-Allen Publishing, Inc., 1994) p. 70.

Hicks, Esther and Jerry, <u>Ask and it is Given, Learning to Manifest your Desires (The Teachings of Abraham)</u>, (Hay House Inc., 2004), p. 109.

Hubbard, Barbara Marx, <u>Emergence, the Shift from Ego to Essence</u>, (Hampton Roads Publishing Company, Inc., 2001), p. 76, 122, 126. 140.

Lisi, Vince, Enlightenment Class, April 29, 2013.

Rasha, <u>Oneness</u>, (Earthstar Press, 2003), p. 22, 52, 69.

Thich Nhat Hanh, <u>Present Moment, Wonderful Moment, Mindfulness Verses for Daily Living</u>, (Parallax Press, 1990), p. 29.

Chapter Four

<u>A Course in Miracles</u>, Volume Two, Workbook for Students, (Foundation for Inner Peace, 1975), p. 151.

Chopra, Deepak, Chopra Center Meditation, Oprah and Deepak's 21-Day Meditation Experience, Desire and Destiny, Day 11, 2014.

Hay, Louise, I Can Do It, How to Use Affirmations to Change Your Life CD.

Hay Louise, <u>You Can Heal Your Life</u>, (Hay House, Inc, 1999), p. 157.

Hicks, Esther and Jerry, <u>Ask and it is Given, Learning to Manifest your Desires (The Teachings of Abraham)</u>, (Hay House Inc., 2004), p. 36.

Hubbard, Barbara Marx, <u>Emergence, the Shift from Ego to Essence</u>, (Hampton Roads Publishing Company, Inc., 2001), p. 64, 74.

Lisi, Vince, Enlightenment Class, February 3, 2014, July 7, 2014, March 9, 2015.

Lisi, Vince, Talk Given at Unity Spiritual Center - Westlake, Ohio, January 5, 2014.

Rasha, <u>Oneness</u>, (Earthstar Press, 2003), p. 22, 76, 147, 148.

Zukav, Gary, <u>Seat of the Soul</u>, (Fireside, Simon and Schuster, 1990), p. 85.

Chapter Five

Hicks, Esther and Jerry, <u>Ask and it is Given, Learning to Manifest your Desires (The Teachings of Abraham)</u>, (Hay House Inc., 2004), p. 109.

Hubbard, Barbara Marx, <u>Emergence, the Shift from Ego to Essence</u>, (Hampton Roads Publishing Company, Inc., 2001), p. 46, 73, 75, 88, 131.

Rasha, <u>Oneness</u>, (Earthstar Press, 2003), p. 148.

Zukav, Gary, <u>Seat of the Soul</u>, (Fireside, Simon and Schuster, 1990), p. 128.

Appendix

<u>A Course in Miracles</u>, Volume Two, Workbook for Students, (Foundation for Inner Peace, 1975), p. 151.

Hicks, Esther and Jerry, <u>Ask and it is Given, Learning to Manifest your Desires (The Teachings of Abraham)</u>, (Hay House Inc., 2004), p. 34, 308, 310, 311.

Lisi, Vince, Talk Given at Unity Spiritual Center - Westlake, Ohio, January 5, 2014.

Lisi, Vince, Thoughts of the Day, January 18, 2014.

Zukav, Gary, <u>Seat of the Soul</u>, (Fireside, Simon and Schuster, 1990), p. 31, 85.

Oneness Circle Notes

Hubbarb, Barbara Marx, <u>Emergence, the Shift from Ego to Essence</u>, (Hampton Roads Publishing company, Inc., 2010), p. 81.

ONENESS CIRCLE NOTES

"The key now is to use profound affirmations continually all day."
Barbara Marx Hubbard

Oneness Circle Notes

Date: _____

My Miracles & Manifestations	My Prompts	My Affirmations

I extend loving energy to the following people:

Oneness Circle Notes

Date: _____

My Miracles & Manifestations	My Prompts	My Affirmations

I extend loving energy to the following people:

Oneness Circle Notes

Date: _____

My Miracles & Manifestations	My Prompts	My Affirmations

I extend loving energy to the following people:

Oneness Circle Notes

Date: _____

My Miracles & Manifestations	My Prompts	My Affirmations

I extend loving energy to the following people:

Oneness Circle Notes

Date: _____

My Miracles & Manifestations	My Prompts	My Affirmations

I extend loving energy to the following people:

Oneness Circle Notes

Date: _____

My Miracles & Manifestations	My Prompts	My Affirmations

I extend loving energy to the following people:

Oneness Circle Notes

Date: _____

My Miracles & Manifestations	My Prompts	My Affirmations

I extend loving energy to the following people:

Oneness Circle Notes

Date: _____

My Miracles & Manifestations	My Prompts	My Affirmations

I extend loving energy to the following people:

Oneness Circle Notes

Date: _____

My Miracles & Manifestations	My Prompts	My Affirmations

I extend loving energy to the following people:

Oneness Circle Notes

Date: _____

My Miracles & Manifestations	My Prompts	My Affirmations

I extend loving energy to the following people: